Faith Without Borders

What does God say about
the borders you set?

By Timothy Reigle
© 2025

Faith Without Borders

Self Published
By Tim Reigle
©2025
All Rights Reserved

ISBN 979-8-218-70339-4

Dedicated To
My Loving Mother
Frances Jean Reigle

Thank you for planting the first seeds

of Faith in my heart.

I am looking forward to seeing you in Heaven.

Table of Contents

Chapter 1 -Borders. 1

Chapter 2 -In the beginning 3

Chapter 3 -Let The Battles begin 7

Chapter 4 -The Battle Moves To Earth 11

Chapter 5 -Man Vs Man 15

Chapter 6 -Borders, Borders and More Borders 19

Chapter 7 -The Borders Move In Closer. 23

Chapter 8 -It Starts With Personal Space 25

Chapter 9 -All Guards Down. 29

Chapter 10 -Once Bitten Twice Shy? Or Not 33

Chapter 11 -What is different About Faith in God?. . . 37

Chapter 12 -What About Faith in Others. 41

Chapter 13 -So How Do We Get Faith? 45

Chapter 14 -Getting In Touch With God 49

Chapter 15 -God's Border Management. 53

Chapter 16 -Our Border Management 57

Chapter 17 -It's About Defense Vs Respect 63

Chapter 18 -Bringing it Home. 67

Chapter 19 -How Can it Be? 71

Chapter 20 -Just Believe. 73

Chapter 21 -My Sins Are Greater Than I. 77

Chapter 22 -Let's Wrap It Up 79

faith

noun
1. complete trust or confidence in someone or something.
    "this restores one's faith in God"
2. strong belief in God or in the doctrines of a religion, based on spiritual apprehension rather than earthly proof.
    "people who have shown supreme faith"

without

preposition
1. in the absence of.
    "he went to Sweden without her"
border

noun
1. a line separating two political or geographical areas, especially countries.
    "they are on border patrol"
2. the edge or boundary of something, or the part near it.
    the border of their distribution area

verb
form an edge along or beside (something).

'Since there is a direct coalition between borders and boundaries I will include the below definition.

boundry

noun
1. a line that marks the limits of an area; a dividing line.
    "the eastern boundary of the wilderness"
2. a limit of a subject or sphere of activity.
    "a community without class or political boundaries"

Because of the relationship between border(s) and boundary(ries) I will use these two words interchangeably.

— Chapter 1 —

Borders

We all have borders. The land you rent or own has its borders. The town you live in or the county your town is in has borders. Then of course a county is in a state, and states make up our country. The world is made up of countries which all have borders. These borders set up areas that give us comfort. We feel protected. Our boundaries are a line that others should not cross. When your borders are crossed, it sometimes gives you the feeling that you need to stand up to protect them. It's this need to protect our borders that are the cause of almost all arguments, battles and wars. This need to protect goes beyond physical borders, It's also a right to the space you "own" around you known as personal boundaries. According to Berkeley.edu "Personal boundaries are the limits and rules you set for ourselves within relationships. A person with healthy boundaries can say "no" to others when they want to, but they are also comfortable opening themselves up to intimacy and close relationships."
https://uhs.berkeley.edu/sites/default/files/relationships_personal_boundaries.pdf

Are Borders needed?
What if you could knock these borders down? Get rid of these lines that have been made in the world, and you have made around you. What if you could just knock them down and we all just get along. Now I'm not suggesting some sort of "one world order" or something, just that there was some sort of understanding of each other's space. Some sort of respect for others' outer limits. Even

this assumes some sort of border or boundary, but it is out of respect not a line drawn out of some sort of space or a right that needs to be protected.

Let's look at this idea for a minute. So there are no borders, but there is an understanding that you have your own spaces. Is there really a difference? Let's look at this later. First, let's look at the history of borders so that you have a better understanding of the when, why and who of them.

— Chapter 2 —

In the beginning

Let's go back in time to look at the first borders ever set up. How far back do you think you'd have to go? Well let's go back there now.

So if you want to see the first time there were borders you have to go to the beginning. How far back is that you might ask. Well, "the beginning", in Genesis.

Genesis 1:1–2
The Creation of the World

> [1] In the beginning, God created the heavens and the earth. [2] The earth was without form and void, and darkness was over the face of the deep. And the Spirit of God was hovering over the face of the waters.

He later in Genesis 1:7 separated the two and this put a border between them.

> [7] And God made the expanse and separated the waters that were under the expanse from the waters that were above the expanse. And it was so.

Since that time borders have been put up everywhere. From countries to states to counties to cities, towns and villages to the property your home is on. There are borders all around you and all around the world.

Borders began before man and to date are still being added and changed. From Genesis 1 to Revelations 22 there are borders.

Genesis 1:3–5

[3] And God said, "Let there be light," and there was light. [4] And God saw that the light was good. And God separated the light from the darkness. [5] God called the light Day, and the darkness he called Night. And there was evening and there was morning, the first day.

Genesis 1:6–8

[6] And God said, "Let there be an expanse in the midst of the waters, and let it separate the waters from the waters." [7] And God made the expanse and separated the waters that were under the expanse from the waters that were above the expanse. And it was so. [8] And God called the expanse Heaven. And there was evening and there was morning, the second day.

The above references are just a few of the borders God has put in place as He created the heavens and the earth. There are also borders that separate Man from Man. This is because as Man started spreading out in the world they gained skills to manage the resources available to them where they ended up. Google AI explains why these borders were likely put in place. "The first borders on Earth were likely established due to the development of early civilizations, where people began to claim territory for agriculture and resource management, often using natural features like rivers, mountains, or forests as dividing lines, as these provided a readily identifiable boundary and limited expansion into neighboring areas; essentially, the need to control territory for survival and prosperity drove the creation of these early borders."

Genesis 14:6

[6] and the Horites in their hill country of Seir as far as Elparan on the border of the wilderness.

Genesis 49:13

[13] "Zebulun shall dwell at the shore of the sea; he shall become a haven for ships, and his border shall be at Sidon.

Revelation 22:18–19

[18] I warn everyone who hears the words of the prophecy of this book: if anyone adds to them, God will add to him the plagues described in this book, [19] and if anyone takes away from the words of the book of this prophecy, God will take away his share in the tree of life and in the holy city, which are described in this book.

Here God has put a border around His word. He also lets you know what happens if you encroach His border. If anyone dares add to or take away from His word they will lose their share in the tree of life.

— Chapter 3 —

Let The Battles begin

So there is the heavens, and there is earth, Between them there is a border. The earth has its space and the heavens have its space. Well if you are a Christian you know that after Satan challenged God and was sent to the depths of the fiery pit, He also gave him dominion over all the earth. So there you have it, the first border that caused a battle and an example of what happens when you challenge God. Let's go into more detail about this. Revelations gives you the details of this battle.

Revelation 12:7-8
Satan Thrown Down to Earth

> [7] Now war arose in heaven, Michael and his angels fighting against the dragon. And the dragon and his angels fought back, [8] but he was defeated, and there was no longer any place for them in heaven.

Rev 12:9 tells you what was done with Satan.

Revelation 12:9

> 9] And the great dragon was thrown down, that ancient serpent who is called the devil and Satan, the deceiver of the whole world—he was thrown down to the earth, and his angels were thrown down with him.

There is now Satan down on the earth with an army of his angels and of course God in heaven with his angels. This is the start of the battle of "good and evil" mentioned in the book of Genesis. This put up the personal border between God and Satan and the used the physical boundary between Heaven and Earth to separate them. So as you can see, even God has battles. But His battles are for your good. When Satan or his angels try to attack us, He steps in and fights the battle for you. That is if you don't try to handle it for yourselves. But you also see that He always wins. God wins every time. The book of Isaiah tells you why He always wins.

Isaiah 55:8–9

> [8] For my thoughts are not your thoughts, neither are your ways my ways, declares the LORD. [9] For as the heavens are higher than the earth, so are my ways higher than your ways and my thoughts than your thoughts.

His thoughts are limitless. He knows what you are going to do before you even think about it. In fact he knew it before the beginning of time. Ephesians 1 tells you this.

Ephesians 1:3–4
Spiritual Blessings in Christ

> [3] Blessed be the God and Father of our Lord Jesus Christ, who has blessed us in Christ with every spiritual blessing in the heavenly places, [4] even as he chose us in him before the foundation of the world, that we should be holy and blameless before him.

Now this does not mean that your whole life is predestined. Just the fact that "he chose us in him". If you continue to read it says:

Ephesians 1:4–6

[4] even as he chose us in him before the foundation of the world, that we should be holy and blameless before him. In love [5] he predestined us for adoption to himself as sons through Jesus Christ, according to the purpose of his will, [6] to the praise of his glorious grace, with which he has blessed us in the Beloved.

So the part of us that might be considered predestined is His choice to select us, who are chosen, "according to the purpose of his will." Those who are chosen, are all of man kind. All you need to do is choose Him back. God battles for you every day, all day. God will not stop until He wins the final battle for you to live with Him in eternity. His desire is for all mankind to make this choice.

— Chapter 4 —

The Battle Moves To Earth

So some time after the creation of earth and the creation of "Man" is the most logical time that satan and his angels were sent to earth. That does not mean that the heavenly battle between God and Satan did not start earlier than that and as you will learn more about later on, it is a battle that is still going on today.

The next battle which would appear to be between Satan and man but was still also between heaven and earth. Satan attempted to show God that he was greater than Him. After man and woman were created, Satan tempted the woman with the fruit from the "Tree of Good and Evil". God had set a border around this tree. Not a physical border, but a personal space. A type of border we will discuss later in this book. Now this trickery is spelled out in Genesis as well.

Genesis 3:1-3

> [1] Now the serpent was more crafty than any other beast of the field that the LORD God had made. He said to the woman, "Did God actually say, 'You shall not eat of any tree in the garden'?" [2] And the woman said to the serpent, "We may eat of the fruit of the trees in the garden, [3] but God said, 'You shall not eat of the fruit of the tree that is in the midst of the garden, neither shall you touch it, lest you die.'"

He used his craftiness to trick the woman into eating the fruit from the one tree He told the man that he was forbidden to eat from. One thing to notice in Genesis 2 is that God commanded the man only. Another thing to notice is that the woman added to what God told man. She added, "neither shall you touch it, lest you die." Do you think that Adam might have added this to make sure she didn't eat this fruit. He felt the need to add his own spin on it. Or could it be that Eve added this in an attempt to show importance of the fact they were not allowed to eat the fruit. Either way you do not need to add anything to God's words. He says what He says the way He says it for a reason.

Genesis 2:15–17

> [15] The LORD God took the man and put him in the garden of Eden to work it and keep it. [16] And the LORD God commanded the man, saying, "You may surely eat of every tree of the garden, [17] but of the tree of the knowledge of good and evil you shall not eat, for in the day that you eat of it you shall surely die."

This tells you that He told only "man" and not "woman" directly, to not eat the fruit from the forbidden tree. In fact it wasn't until after He told the man not to eat from this tree that God gave the man a helper. So now you know that Adam had to have passed this onto Eve. She did not hear God give this command. This is also shown in Genesis 3. Notice that when Eve is tempted by Satan, she never confirms that she was told by God not to eat the fruit from the Tree of Good and Evil. It would seem as though Eve received this second hand and Satan knew this. In Genesis 3:3 Eve responds "but God said," not that God told us, or me. Again, she also adds to what God had said to Adam when she says "neither shall you touch it, lest you die." This is why I believe Satan chose to trick Eve. If you think about it, it's like getting told of a rule from your co-worker, not your boss. Getting information from a co-worker does not carry as much weight as hearing it from your boss.

Now, even though Satan deceived Eve, it wasn't until Adam ate the fruit from the forbidden tree that sin entered into the picture. Satan knew that once he convinced Eve, that she would be able to seduce Adam into partaking as well. Satan is good at breaking through your borders so you need to keep close to God and under the protection of the borders He has placed around us.

There are many more references throughout the Holy Bible regarding this event that you should consider when studying this topic. 2 Corinthians 11:3 and Romans 5:12-21 are just a couple. You can search most bible apps and websites to find more.

Now, your life is full of battles that are spiritual and are fought for you by God, if you allow him to. It is up to you to have faith in His promises that are spelled out throughout His word, The Holy Bible. Beyond spiritual battles, Man now battles against himself.

— Chapter 5 —

Man Vs Man

Earthly battles among mankind have been going on since early in time and continue to go on today. The first battle amongst humans can be found in Genesis chapter 4. Cain and Abel, both sons of Adam and Eve, had brought God an offering. Cain, who was a worker of the ground, brought an offering of "the fruit of the ground". Abel, who was a keeper of sheep, brought to God an offering of "the first born of his flock". God was pleased with Abel's offering but was not impressed with Cain's. In faith Abel gave his best. "The first born of his flock". Cain did not give his best, that of his first harvest. He did not have faith that if he gave from the first of his harvest that God would provide more. I wonder if he set it aside for himself. What do you think?

Genesis 4:3–5

> [3] In the course of time Cain brought to the LORD an offering of the fruit of the ground, [4] and Abel also brought of the firstborn of his flock and of their fat portions. And the LORD had regard for Abel and his offering, [5] but for Cain and his offering he had no regard. So Cain was very angry, and his face fell.

"His face fell."

It sounds like this affected him alot. When has God done something to you that made your face fall? Now over time Cain got jealous of the praise Abel had received.

Genesis 4:7–8

> [7] If you do well, will you not be accepted? And if you do not do well, sin is crouching at the door. Its desire is contrary to you, but you must rule over it."

In verse 7 God is warning Cain about the sin that is festering inside him. If he lets it go and turns from his sin he will be accepted by God. He will be one of the "chosen". If he does not, sin will overtake him.

Well, the story does not end here.

> [8] Cain spoke to Abel his brother. And when they were in the field, Cain rose up against his brother Abel and killed him.

Now it does not say what Cain said to Abel but chances are he lured his brother into the field. It seems to me that the murder of Abel might have been a premeditated act. Also look at Hebrews 11:4 and 1John 3:11-24.

Since that first battle between these two men, we continue to battle over our spaces and over the temptation to sin and not have faith in God. You can see this in Genesis 14, one of the earlier battles. A battle that probably resulted in changing borders.

Genesis 14:5–6

> [5] In the fourteenth year Chedorlaomer and the kings who were with him came and defeated the Rephaim in Ashteroth-karnaim, the Zuzim in Ham, the Emim in Shaveh-kiriathaim, [6] and the Horites in their hill country of Seir as far as El-paran on the border of the wilderness.

So you can see how when Cheorlaomre and the other

kings went to war because of a rebellion and gained more land it changed their borders.

Today there are still wars going on and we are still battling over our spaces. A funny take I got from this passage is that even the wilderness has its borders.

Since that time battles and wars have been going on over all the earth. The Rule of Law in Armed Conflicts project (RULAC) of the Geneva Academy of International Humanitarian Law and Human Rights, which hosts a unique online portal that identifies and classifies situations of armed conflict. The portal provides information on the parties to these conflicts, and applicable international law. There are more than 110 armed conflicts currently going on around the world as of the writing of this book. Some of these conflicts make the headlines, others do not. Some of them started recently, while others have lasted for more than 50 years.

— Chapter 6 —

Borders, Borders and More Borders

When creating the Garden of Eden, God describes the borders He put in place. He laid it out by using landmarks. Genesis 2 gives you the landmarks used to define the borders of Eden.

Genesis 2:10–14

> [10] A river flowed out of Eden to water the garden, and there it divided and became four rivers. [11] The name of the first is the Pishon. It is the one that flowed around the whole land of Havilah, where there is gold. [12] And the gold of that land is good; bdellium and onyx stone are there. [13] The name of the second river is the Gihon. It is the one that flowed around the whole land of Cush. [14] And the name of the third river is the Tigris, which flows east of Assyria. And the fourth river is the Euphrates.

You will notice that the river which flowed through the Garden of Eden divided into four rivers forming the borders of three lands and the fourth simply flowed from the Garden of Eden and marked what is probably the east border of Assyria. As you now know there are so many borders in this world. According to Worldometers.info "There are 195 countries in the world today. This total comprises 193 countries that are member states of the United Nations and 2 countries that are non-member observer states: the Holy Land (Vatican City) and the State of Palestine." With this, if you consider the lands with these 195 countries that are separated by borders that number grows significantly. Within most of these borders the majority of the people have the same basic beliefs. Whether it's their religious belief, political belief or some other belief. These beliefs are another set of borders.

In the book of Exodus, when the Israelites fled Egypt, God promised them a land flowing with milk and honey. Well they doubted Him so he made them wander in the desert for forty years. When they were finally able to enter their promised land, God set the borders up for them. Some years later, about four hundred years later, in the book of Samuel, the Philistines, who didn't have the same beliefs both culturally and when it came to religion, set up to battle the Israelites over these difference's and over land and border disputes.

In the book of Samuel it talks of one of these battles. Probably one of the most famous battle in the bible and maybe even all of history. This battle had several types of borders that caused it. The Israelites asserted their claim to the land God had promised them in Exodus. They also were not on the same page when it came to religious and cultural beliefs.

1 Samuel 17:1–4
David and Goliath

> [1] Now the Philistines gathered their armies for battle. And they were gathered at Socoh, which belongs to Judah, and encamped between Socoh and Azekah, in Ephes-dammim. [2] And Saul and the men of Israel were gathered, and encamped in the Valley of Elah, and drew up in line of battle against the Philistines. [3] And the Philistines stood on the mountain on the one side, and Israel stood on the mountain on

the other side, with a valley between them.

So you can see that the most famous battle in the bible and maybe even all of history had several types of borders that had caused it.

If you know this bible story you know what happened when someone of great faith finally stepped up.

1 Samuel 17:49

> [49] And David put his hand in his bag and took out a stone and slung it and struck the Philistine on his forehead. The stone sank into his forehead, and he fell on his face to the ground.

David was not even a trained soldier. He was a sheepherder sent to the battle ground to deliver food to his brothers. Take the time to read this whole story in 1 Samuel 16 and 17.

So you can see that the most famous battle in the bible and maybe even all of history had several types of borders that had caused it.

— Chapter 7 —

The Borders Move In Closer

As we become more intelligent and technologically advanced, so does your personal space. Smartphones are your newest type of personal space. As I sit and write this book I mostly sit in a cafe, put my earbuds in and hit play on my Lauren Daigle playlist on my smartphone. I need it by my side all the time. Its personal space is inside my personal space. If it is not within my personal space it's like an underground pet fence. There is a signal sent out to me like you've been shocked in my brain, similar to that of an electric dog collar. Like most people I have put some, if not most, of my life on this thing. Talk about faith. This thing is connected to the world. Literally the whole world...

So you can see how borders are a necessary part of your world. The ESV Bible mentions borders sixty two times. After all, how can you separate countries, states, counties, cities and towns without borders? The same holds true when it comes to personal space. More about that subject in the next chapter. So the question has to be, "how do you live in faith without borders when there are so many of them around you?".

Let's talk about different types of borders.
Personal space. Now most of the time you think this is the space around you that you don't want to be encroached on. Although this is your personal space there is more to it than that. Let's start with your work space. You most likely have made this your space with some, or many, per-

sonal items, like pictures of the lovely family or your favorite coffee mug. Maybe some plants or other things you have added to make it yours.

Physical space. What about your vehicle? You might have rubber duckies lined up across the dashboard or fuzzy dice hanging on the rear view mirror. But it is your space and you have set boundaries. No one dares touch those rubber duckies or fuzzy dice.

Even the outside of your vehicle has its space. It's called Space cushion. When you are driving, if anyone gets too close to you it makes you feel uncomfortable and in some extreme cases this causes road rage. People have lost their life over this personal space. In 2023 alone hundreds of people died over the personal space around their vehicle. These facts and more on this subject are available by simply searching on the Internet.

— Chapter 8 —

It Starts With Personal Space

Personal spaces. When you get home from work or running errands you pull into your driveway to go into your home, emphasis on "your". These are your personal and physical spaces.

So I just sat down at Starbucks to work on this book and there was another customer to my left working on their computer. Their computer bag was on the bench seat between us and as I started to set up I put my computer bag on the bench seat between us as well. The two bags were about eight to ten inches apart, but as I continued to set up they reached over to their bag and pulled it a couple of inches closer to them. I took that action as a message that I needed to maintain a good distance from their personal space. I feel these types of actions are mostly done instinctively. They probably didn't even think about what they had just done. They just possibly felt encroached upon.

That same action could have been translated to let you know that if you needed more space that it was okay to take the couple of inches they moved out of. I translated it to the safest meaning. That way I avoided a possible conflict.

Let's be honest about it. Most of the time people don't say what they feel. This is true because they're afraid that they will hurt someone, or that the other person is going to take them wrong. It's easy to let this fear prevent you from doing what really is the easier thing. If you just take a chance and tell the other person how you really feel about them being in your personal space, most of the time you'll find respect is given back. This is true as long as you present your feelings in a loving manner. You don't always need to say it verbally. Like the gentleman I sat next to, he just made a gesture, either consciously or unconsciously, by moving his computer bag a little closer to himself.

So think about your house and land around it as a country. You have to lead, support and control everything that is going on in the space that you call home. People who step into your personal space have to follow the rules you have made. Now your neighbor has their rules that may not align with yours. They don't like the way you do things so they attack you. In your space. Well, before long there is a battle, and if left unsettled, a war. Almost everyone has probably heard of at least one story of a dispute that started because of some petty thing, like a small encroachment of a property line. If not handled in a caring and loving way then an argument ensues. Before you know it, if not brought under control it may become physical. A fight breaks out and the police get involved. Once this happens it is hard to peddle it back. If it ends up in court because charges have been filed, there is a good chance lawsuits will follow. This often times ends up with one, or both parties involved moving to get away from the situation. That is after the families and friends of both sides end up getting hurt as well. If they had only handled it in a caring and loving way things might not have escalated at all. God in is word tells us to handle these situations in the book of Matthew.

Matthew 5:25–26

[25] Come to terms quickly with your accuser while you are going with him to court, lest your accuser hand you over to the judge, and the judge to the guard, and you be put in prison.

He tells us to talk with the other party before you even get into court. Settle the matter before things get out of hand.

Arguments, disputes, fights and wars have been started over people's personal, physical and geographical spaces. Moreover people have died over something as simple as "my personal space". Fights have started over simple things such as an airplane armrest, a parking space, the space around your vehicle while driving down the road and the land you have rights too.

— Chapter 9 —

All Guards Down

Have you ever let all your guards down? Have you ever met the person, who you hope is the love of your life and let them enter your personal space? Then, as the relationship grows you let them get closer and closer to you. If everything goes well this person will probably get closer to you than even your own family. You might at some point fall head over heels "in love" with them. At this point all walls are easily knocked down. You become extremely vulnerable when this happens. Your shields are down and your life and personal thoughts are wide open for this person to access.

The hope is that this will lead to a long and happy life with this person. But, sometimes this goes wrong. Sometimes this goes really wrong. When this happens it throws your life into a tailspin, nose diving toward the ground to crash into a ball of flames.

In the book of Judges there is the story of Samson. Samson was a man who had great strength. He fell head over heels for a woman named Delilah. Some time later she was offered money, a lot of money, by the Philistines to seduce him and find out where his strength came from. At first Samson told Delilah lies so the source of his strength did not get revealed. After lying to her three times Delilah nagged him day after day until he finally told her the source of his strength.

Judges 16:15

> [15] And she said to him, "How can you say, 'I love you,' when your heart is not with me? You have mocked me these three times, and you have not told me where your great strength lies."

So the story of Samson continues and tells you how bad she nagged him.

Judges 16:16

> [16] And when she pressed him hard with her words day after day, and urged him, his soul was vexed to death.

Vexed to death", WOW. Have you ever been "vexed to death"? The definition of vexed according to the Oxford Dictionary is:

vexed
adjective

1.(of a problem or issue) difficult and much debated; problematic.

"the relationship is becoming strained over the vexed question of money"

So Delilah became "difficult" and "problematic" to Samson so much so that Samson's soul was not simply vexed, but rather "vexed to death". He just wanted her to stop nagging him. Have you ever felt this way about someone?

So after this, Samson finally told her where his strength lay.

Judges 16:17

[17] And he told her all his heart, and said to her, "A razor has never come upon my head, for I have been a Nazirite to God from my mother's womb. If my head is shaved, then my strength will leave me, and I shall become weak and be like any other man."

You can look up what a Nazirite is in Numbers chapter 6.

He gave away his secret, the source of his strength. He trusted her. And what did she do? Well she did the one thing that would cause him to lose what God had given him through a vow. She chopped his hair off so she could collect her money from the philistines. Lust got the best of him. He feared losing his wife, the love of his life. He did not trust God to protect him. Sin got the best of her because she allowed someone to encroach into her personal space. Greed had gotten a hold of her.

— Chapter 10 —

Once Bitten Twice Shy? Or Not

I think that it is important to note that this was not the first time Samson had a wife and was taken advantage of by her. His first wife nagged him as well and got him to tell her the answer to a riddle he presented to some uninvited guests who came to his feast. This cost him then as well.

Judges 14:14–16

[14] And he said to them

> "Out of the eater came something to eat.
>
> Out of the strong came something sweet."

And in three days they could not solve the riddle. [15] On the fourth day they said to Samson's wife, "Entice your husband to tell us what the riddle is, lest we burn you and your father's house with fire. Have you invited us here to impoverish us?" [16] And Samson's wife wept over him and said, "You only hate me; you do not love me. You have put a riddle to my people, and you have not told me what it is." And he said to her, "Behold, I have not told my father nor my mother, and shall I tell you?"

If you want to know the answer to the riddle you can read this story in Judges 14:10-18. It seems he did not learn from his mistakes very well.

This is what happens if you let your guard down with

things of this earth. When you fall head over heels for someone, or have a lifelong friend that you trust or a co-worker you depend on. When you trust someone or have faith in them, a faith that they have your best interests in hand. Faith that they will never hurt you. This is why you need to know the wisdom from reading God's word. By receiving this wisdom you see that true faith can only come from the Lord your God. You would trust that He, through The Holy Spirit, leads you and trust that He has your best interest in hand. Always and in All Ways.

On the flip side you also might find that you need to push in on someone's borders to knock them down so you can reveal the truth from their heart. Knocking down the walls that are blocking the light from getting in will allow sins to be revealed. Sin can not hide in the light.

In the movie "A Few Good Men" Colonel Jessup, played by Jack Nicholson, is being interrogated by Lieutenant Kaffee, played by Tom Cruise, about an incident that took place on Colonel Jessup's base. He's trying to get the Colonel to admit that he ordered other soldiers to give what he considers a weak link a "Code Red" which causes his death. Kaffee keeps pushing into the wall and Jessup pushes back, but eventually loses it. When he does, it causes his wall to crumble.

"Son, we live in a world that has walls. And those walls have to be guarded by men with guns. Who's gonna do it? You? You, Lt. Weinberg? I have a greater responsibility than you can possibly fathom. You weep for Santiago and you curse the marines. You have that luxury. You have the luxury of not knowing what I know: That Santiago's death, while tragic, probably saved lives. And my existence, while grotesque and incomprehensible to you, saves lives.

You don't want the truth. Because deep down, in places you don't talk about at parties, you want me on that wall. You need me there. We use words like honor, code, loyalty. We use these words as the backbone to a life spent defending something. You use 'em as a punchline. I have neither the time nor the inclination to explain myself to a man who rises and sleeps under the blanket of the very freedom I provide, then questions the manner in which I provide it. I'd prefer you just said thank you and went on your way. Otherwise, I suggest you pick up a weapon and stand a post. Either way, I don't give a damn what you think you're entitled to."

Jessup allowed his anger to get the best of him and as the interrogation continues he admits that he did in fact order the "Code Red"

— Chapter 11 —

What is different About Faith in God?

First let's take another look at what faith really is. To understand what faith is you can look in the book of Hebrews,

Hebrews 11:1

> [1] Now faith is the assurance of things hoped for, the conviction of things not seen.

Faith is important. Very important. Faith also goes hand in hand with trust. These two concepts have a symbiotic or reciprocal like relationship. Can you have faith in something or someone if you don't have trust? Faith is important here on earth because without it you would never sit down or work with anyone or have relations with others. There has to be faith or nothing would ever get accomplished. How could you go to work and believe that those you work with will do their part if you did not have some faith and trust in them? Trust is an action based on faith. All throughout the bible this theme can be found. Noah had faith in God so when God told him to build a giant boat he trusted Him and did as he was told.

First and foremost God gives you His word that He will always be faithful. This promise is in the book of Exodus.

Exodus 34:6

> [6] The LORD passed before him and proclaimed, "The LORD, the LORD, a God merciful and gracious, slow to anger, and abounding in steadfast love and

faithfulness,

So He is "abounding in steadfast love and faithfulness". Faith in God is based on the trust of someone you can't look at in the face, reach out and shake a hand, or carry on a verbal conversation with. This is not to say you can't see the face of God, feel God's touch or speak to and listen to God. You can see that the faith you have in God is much different than the faith you have in the things on earth. Your faith in God goes far beyond the faith you have with anything or anyone on earth. Or at least it should.

How can you have faith in something or someone you cans see. Well you can't see the wind but you know it is there. You know it's there because you can feel the effects it makes all around us. The same holds true about your faith in God.

So where does faith in God come from? You can find this is laid out in the book of Romans.

Romans 10:17

> [17] So faith comes from hearing, and hearing through the word of Christ. .

2 Timothy tells you how you can know God's faithfulness in you even when you fall short.

2 Timothy 2:11-13

> 11 The saying is trustworthy, for: If we have died with him, we will also live with him; 12 if we endure, we will also reign with him; if we deny him, he also will deny us; 13 if we are faithless, he remains faithful—for he cannot deny himself.

The first two statements are based on steps you take. The third statement is a choice you take to reject Him. In the final one you see that even if you are not faithful He is. You can fail in your faith in Him but He will still have complete faith in you. Without His faithfulness we cannot build our faith. He is the rock we build our faith with. He can't be unfaithful. It's just not who He is.

Build you faith on Him as a foundation

The Master Chef.

So imagine that you go to your favorite restaurant to order your favorite plate. The chef looks out the little round kitchen door window. He sees you their and knows what plate you're going to order. He sends for you to be brought into the kitchen. He tells you that he is going to let you watch him prepare your meal. As he is adding and mixing some spices you say to him that maybe he should add just a pinch more salt. He turns and gives you a quick look and continues preparing the food. As he continues the work on your plate you suggest maybe the fire is to low. He gives you another look, this time a little longer and with question on his face. A little while later as he turns the meat over and adjusts the heat a little, you say "maybe it will cook faster if you turn the heat up." He looks at you again and says,"You think so." You say, "Yes, it will also give you more time to tend to others meals." He looks at you and says, "Oh okay, I'll tell you what. I'll go stand over there and watch you finish it yourself." "Okay," you say with excitement. "Thanks" and you take over the cooking. You turn the heat up so you can sit and enjoy the mouth watering meal as quickly as possible. The next thing you know is that the pan is smoking and you see that the food has over cooked. You look over at the chef and they simply say to you, "Would you like me to do it for you now?" "Yes," you respond. "Forgive me for not trusting you. I now have full faith that you will make it correctly."

How many times have you done this when God is doing something for you? When has He not been there to correct the things that you have messed up?

— Chapter 12 —

What About Faith in Others

You also need to have faith in others, even when they do not have faith in you, just like God's faith in you when your faith is lacking. When you have faith in others it is really having faith in God, even if you don't trust them or feel that having faith in them is the best idea. You need to know that God's got you.

Now, it is a little more complicated than that. The book of Romans, according to the ESV Global Study Bible is --

"The global message of Romans is that all people everywhere have free access to the riches of God's grace in Christ as they respond in faith to the gospel. In his own Son, God has made a way for lost people to be restored to him—lost people whether they are Greeks or barbarians, wise or foolish."

So let's digest all that for a minute. You have to "respond in faith to the gospel" then you can begin to gain knowledge. There is that word "faith" again. It is found 257 times in the ESV bible and a total of 422 times if you count other forms of the word like faithful, faithfulness and unfaithful, etc.. It seems to be pretty important if it is mentioned that many times.

To do this properly you can start by reading the text as it is written in Romans 14.

Romans 14:1–4

Do Not Pass Judgment on One Another

[1] As for the one who is weak in faith, welcome him, but not to quarrel over opinions. [2] One person believes he may eat anything, while the weak person eats only vegetables. [3] Let not the one who eats despise the one who abstains, and let not the one who abstains pass judgment on the one who eats, for God has welcomed him. [4] Who are you to pass judgment on the servant of another? It is before his own master that he stands or falls. And he will be upheld, for the Lord is able to make him stand.

So this passage in Romans 14 tells you to welcome those who are weak in faith. Help them to grow in their faith by sharing God's Word lovingly with them. It also tells you to not argue with them over your differences but instead to have faith in God. Like it says, "For the Lord is able to make them stand." Faith is key throughout the entire book of Romans. Now this does not mean that you are to just trust everyone completely. You are warned of this in Proverbs 12.

Proverbs 12:5

[5] The thoughts of the righteous are just; the counsels of the wicked are deceitful.

And also Proverbs 25.

Proverbs 25:19

[19] Trusting in a treacherous man in time of trouble is like a bad tooth or a foot that slips.

So I take from these verses to mean that you are to watch out because "the wicked are deceitful." and be careful of dealing with "a treacherous man in time of trouble" In both these cases you are putting yourself out there to be taken advantage of and pulled down into a pit. Instead look to God in Faith to guide you through the Holy Spirit.

You are told in Proverbs 1 how you can protect yourself from getting deceived or pulled down.

Proverbs 1:2–6

> [2] To know wisdom and instruction, to understand words of insight, [3] to receive instruction in wise dealing, in righteousness, justice, and equity; [4] to give prudence to the simple, knowledge and discretion to the youth— [5] Let the wise hear and increase in learning, and the one who understands obtain guidance, [6] to understand a proverb and a saying, the words of the wise and their riddles

So you have to "know wisdom" and receive "instruction in wise dealing" from God to protect yourself. This passage also tells you that you need to have "increase in learning" and for the "one who understands obtain guidance". That does not mean that you can't or shouldn't seek counsel, it means to take counsel from other brothers in Christ. Then, lay it before the Lord to guide you the rest of the way

— Chapter 13 —

So How Do You Get Faith?

Faith has to be present in those who are sent out to preach the word. Their job is to preach the good word and trust or have faith that God is going to work on the hearts of those who hear and those who don't. That can also be found in Romans. It tells you they have to have faith.

Romans 10:13–17

> [13] For "everyone who calls on the name of the Lord will be saved." [14] How then will they call on him in whom they have not believed? And how are they to believe in him of whom they have never heard? And how are they to hear without someone preaching? [15] And how are they to preach unless they are sent? As it is written, "How beautiful are the feet of those who preach the good news!" [16] But they have not all obeyed the gospel. For Isaiah says, "Lord, who has believed what he has heard from us?" [17] So faith comes from hearing, and hearing through the word of Christ.

In the passage above, God is being questioned by His disciples about what good their preaching is doing and who is even listening. God responds with "As it is written, "How beautiful are the feet of those who preach the good news!'" He says "How beautiful are the feet" because they walked everywhere they went back then. Today He might say How beautiful the wheels are , LOL. So God reminds them how their good works are what is important and He will take care of those who are really listening as well as those who are not hearing what is preached. The end of this passage is the bullseye of the whole thing about faith. Verse [17] says "So faith comes from hearing, and hearing through the word of Christ."

So you have to hear and read the Word of God. From this you will both gain and grow in your faith in God. A faith like no other. A faith far beyond anything you can imagine. A faith that will never ever let you down. Having this faith will allow you to have more faith in those you need to depend on. But most people have built a wall around what they believe and won't let the words spoken by those who preach the gospel, or what they might read, enter their space. They don't want to hear the truth. They don't have faith in God.

The book of Hebrews tells you just how important it is to have faith in God.

Hebrews 11:6

> [6] And without faith it is impossible to please him, for whoever would draw near to God must believe that he exists and that he rewards those who seek him.

Now that is important. To think that it is "impossible to please Him" without faith. Do you think that this could be the difference between Cain's offering and Abel's offering?

You can also see in the book of Peter that faith is priceless.

1 Peter 1:6–7

> [6] In this you rejoice, though now for a little while,

if necessary, you have been grieved by various trials, [7] so that the tested genuineness of your faith—more precious than gold that perishes though it is tested by fire—may be found to result in praise and glory and honor at the revelation of Jesus Christ.

"More precious than gold" You are also told that faith is more valuable than the most precious thing on earth. Like gold, your faith in God is also tested, put to the fire like gold, so it can be made pure. The trials that you go through are the purifying fires that are gifts from God. He uses them to test and purify your faith in Him.

At the basic level, here on earth faith is pretty simple. You have faith every day. Every time you sit down in a chair you do so in faith. You have faith that it was designed and constructed properly so that when you sit in it, it will not collapse. It will not let you down. Literally.

You have faith in your co-workers and boss that they will have your back. You have faith that they will be there when you need them. There is an activity to help you build your faith in others. You would have someone stand behind you and with your eyes closed, you fall back. You have to have faith in them to catch you and not let you hit the floor. Faith that they are there for you.

Examples of faith you hold are in the chair you sit in every day and in the faith you have in the person who needs to be there to catch you when you need them. You are pretty sure that the chair you sit in everyday will not collapse. You know when someone is standing behind you and you trust them to catch you. You have faith in the person behind you on the road that you have never met. You have faith that they are going to stop behind you when the light changes, instead of running into you because you stopped for it. You have faith that when someone tells you something that what they are saying is true. There are many other things and people that you have faith in. In Fact the list might be almost endless. But these are all things you can physically see, hear or touch.

— Chapter 14 —

Getting In Touch With God

God on the other hand you can not see, hear or touch like those things on earth. You just have faith in Him and all that He says He is. Well, actually you can see, hear and feel the touch of God, just not like those things of earth.

If you seek Him out you will see Him in the help you receive from the Helper that He sent you. You can see this in John 14

John 14:26

> [26] But the Helper, the Holy Spirit, whom the Father will send in my name, he will teach you all things and bring to your remembrance all that I have said to you.

"bring to your remembrance all that I have said to you". This is an important statement because it tells you that you have to know what he has said then He can "bring to your remembrance", or remind you what He has said to you. To know what He has said you have to know His Word because His Word gives you the guidance you need to live out the will of God. You know what He has said by reading and hearing the bible. This passage also tells you that when you start to get off track the Holy Spirit steps in and touches your heart. He "whispers" into your heart to remind you what His word has told you. Your faith in the Gospel Truth will help you be willing to adjust yourself back on track. This is like the little lights in the side view mirrors on your car and the alarm that sounds when you want to turn or change lanes when there is a car in your blind spot. This lets you know that if you do what you are thinking of doing you will be in trouble. It keeps you in your lane and protects you just like The Holy Spirit does in your heart. God will speak to you louder as you get closer to sin, or are lacking in faith like the alarm on your car when you put it in reverse. As you are backing up the beeps get closer and shorter until it sounds continuously. At that point if you keep backing up you will hit whatever is behind you..

You hear Him by reading His word and listening to the lessons taught at church service, home group or bible study. You can see this in the book of Romans 10.

Romans 10:14–15

> [14] How then will they call on him in whom they have not believed? And how are they to believe in him of whom they have never heard? And how are they to hear without someone preaching? [15] And how are they to preach unless they are sent? As it is written, "How beautiful are the feet of those who preach the good news!"

You can see here the importance of those who preach God's word. One part of this passage stands out to me. "And how are they to hear without someone preaching?" So if the preacher is important then you need to hear what is preached from His Word, The Holy Bible. This will help you to grow in your faith in God.

As you can see, I have used this passage twice. Each time to make a different point.

The Holy Bible is also called the living word. It tells you this in Hebrews 4.

Hebrews 4:12

[12] For the word of God is living and active, sharper than any two-edged sword, piercing to the division of soul and of spirit, of joints and of marrow, and discerning the thoughts and intentions of the heart.

So through The Holy Bible you hear God speaking to you. You see here that it is "living and active". His words have meaning based on what you are going through. I have used the same passage in Romans 10 to bring to point several different ideas. You may also read Psalm 72:12-14 and go out and help those who are in need. You may find yourself in need and read this same passage and be more comfortable and willing to ask for help.

Psalm 71:12

[12] O God, be not far from me; O my God, make haste to help me!

In these situations God speaks to you but in different ways. They are the same passages but because they are a part of His living word they help those who hear them differently.

God's touch can be felt when He touches your heart. Those whose hearts He touches become renewed. It changes who you are. You can see this in 1 Samuel.

1 Samuel 10:26

[26] Saul also went to his home at Gibeah, and with him went men of valor whose hearts God had

touched.

In this passage Samuel had anointed Saul as king of the Jews. Samuel sent all the people away to their homes. Saul was accompanied by others whose hearts had been "touched by God. This made them "men of valor"

This touch by God brought on something good, but sometimes God's touch brings you suffering. You see this in 2 Kings.

2 Kings 15:4–5

> [4] Nevertheless, the high places were not taken away. The people still sacrificed and made offerings on the high places. [5] And the LORD touched the king, so that he was a leper to the day of his death, and he lived in a separate house. And Jotham the king's son was over the household, governing the people of the land.

Here Saul had not stopped the people from trying to be atoned for their sins by sacrificing and making offerings, the old way, or to false gods. Before Christ gave His life for this purpose. This touch from God brought on suffering. Sometimes God brings on good and if you live out His word then good is what you will see. God brings on suffering to guide you back to Him or to teach you to rely on Him. Either way it is good. Do you think that Saul learned a lesson? Do you think that Saul relied on God for the rest of his life? If not, who do you think might be willing to care for a leper?

So now you know that you can see, hear and feel God. This is where your faith will shine. By believing in Him and having faith in God.

— Chapter 15 —

God's Border Management

To get an idea of God's border management you can look throughout the bible. Let's look at one story that shows an example of this. You will find it in the Book of Job. If you are not familiar with it, God's word tells us about Job and I think you should really take the time to read his story. It starts out in Job 1:1 by telling you just what type of person Job was and what God gave to him because of his faith.

Job 1:1

Job's Character and Wealth

> [1] There was a man in the land of Uz whose name was Job, and that man was blameless and upright, one who feared God and turned away from evil.

Job was also very rich. Not only with possessions but also with family and friends.

Job 1:2–3

> [2] There were born to him seven sons and three daughters. [3] He possessed 7,000 sheep, 3,000 camels, 500 yoke of oxen, and 500 female donkeys, and very many servants, so that this man was the greatest of all the people of the east.

"The greatest of all" Wow! It would seem that Job had no need for borders. I think that because of Jobs faith, God put His border around him. God surrounded him with a hedge of protection. Everyone would look up to a man of such great stature. Can you think of anyone today who might stand as tall as Job must have? Who do you think Job gave thanks to for all he had achieved?

So anyways, Satan was allowed to test Job. He was allowed to encroach on Jobs' borders by God. One by one Satan was allowed to knocked down the borders around Job's life that God had made. God had to allow this or Satan wouldn't have been able to do it. He had such faith in Job that He was sure his faith would withstand the testing by Satan's deeds. To find out why God allowed it you'll have to read the Book of Job.

Now when Satan was given the okay to test Job's faith in God He only placed one restriction on the borders that Satan was allowed to inflict on Job. He was not allowed to lay a finger on Job himself. So, Satan took Job's livestock and servants. He then took his children and destroyed his property, crumbling his buildings to rubble with his family inside.

What is the worst thing that has ever happened to you? How do you think you would respond if all of this were to happen to you?

Now that you know the backstory I'll get to my point. Job continued to trust and have faith in God, even after he lost everything. He pleaded with God to take away the suffering he was going through Having the faith to know that God would not leave or forsake him. Even though the suffering was so great that he wished he had never been born.

Job 3:1–4

Job Laments His Birth

[1] After this Job opened his mouth and cursed the day of his birth. [2] And Job said: [3] "Let the day perish on which I was born, and the night that said, 'A man is conceived.' [4] Let that day be darkness! May God above not seek it, nor light shine upon it and loathing his life.

Job 10:1
Job Continues: A Plea to God

[1] "I loathe my life; I will give free utterance to my complaint; I will speak in the bitterness of my soul.

Have you ever wished you were never born? Earlier in the story, when things had just started to turn sour, even his wife encouraged him to ask God to take his life. Imagine your spouse asking you to die. I don't think she said this to get rid of him. She probably couldn't take seeing the man she loved suffer any more. Maybe she did lose her integrity lie Job mentions in Job 2:9. She was like 'why bother' it's not going to get better.

Job 2:9

[9] Then his wife said to him, "Do you still hold fast your integrity? Curse God and die."

Through all this Job never lost faith in God. He did not let borders get between him and God. Now this is an example of the faith without borders that you should have.

Now God saw that Job remained faithful and that he had had enough.

So starting in Chapter 38 God answers Job. He does this by describing His borders and laying out His boundaries. He reminds Job just how great He really is. He does this by asking Job a series of questions.

Job 38:4–5

> [4] "Where were you when I laid the foundation of the earth? Tell me, if you have understanding. [5] Who determined its measurements—surely you know! Or who stretched the line upon it?

This line of questioning continues through Chapter 41 and includes 62 questions in total. Each question is designed to show Job just how powerful God really is. To show him that He has no borders. Now that does not mean that He doesn't have, and sets limits but those are set for your sake. He uses them to guide us and keep us in check. God shows you here that He has no borders. After all He is the creator of all things. He owns everything, everywhere so He has no need for borders.

Wait just one minute you might be thinking right about now, I thought that in chapter 3 you said that God did set up borders. You would be correct. The Bible says in Genesis 1:1 "In the beginning God created the heavens and the earth." He later in Genesis 1:7 separated the two and this put a border between them. God did put borders in place, but these are for us. He doesn't need them, you do. The border between Heaven and earth keeps our atmosphere enclosed around earth. You need this to survive. Every border, as I stated in the previous paragraph, God puts in place is for your good. God has no need for them.

— Chapter 16 —

Our Border Management

So the title of this book is "Faith Without Borders", as you know. We first looked at borders. We then looked at the Faith portion of this. Now let's look at Better Border Management and then discuss how you can live out your life having Faith Without Borders. After all, if you're too busy fighting over borders, how can you find enough time to build relationships?

Better border management begins with first better understanding your borders and boundaries. You need to have a reasonable idea of the limits you have and be willing to mark them without stirring things up. How do others respond to the borders you have set up? Reasonable borders will almost always get reasonable results. For the most part, other people do not purposely encroach on another person's personal space for example. It is either assumed to be okay or accidentally crossed in to. Either way someone is probably going to feel uncomfortable. Although the person entering your space may realize that they have crossed into your space it is normally the person who is being encroached upon that first feels uncomfortable. As the personal boundary is encroached upon more and more, the person being encroached upon feels more uncomfortable. The more the border is crossed the higher the level of discomfort. At some point it will cause the person to feel uncomfortable enough to react. That reaction can determine how the other person responds. And if it goes on and on a conflict can start. A conflict turns into a battle and battles can turn into wars. For this reason you are told to ask for forgiveness. In fact God does not even want us to pay homage to him until you have done this. This is told to us in Matthew 5.

Matthew 5:23-24

> [23] So if you are offering your gift at the altar and there remember that your brother has something against you, [24] leave your gift there before the altar and go. First be reconciled to your brother, and then come and offer your gift.

God wants you to come before Him with a clean heart. After all how can you stand before the creator of all things, the most high, the one who breathed the first breath into your lungs to ask for forgiveness when you yourself are not cleansed.

Now, once you understand your borders you need to learn how to let others know when they are getting too close. As you get better at this you find it easier to do. Learning to protect your borders is not always possible. In the cases of the borders you set around you or your personal property you can learn to control how close others get. Spaces like those directly around you or the space in your office or cubicle at work are easier to control than those like the space around your vehicle while you are driving.

So let's start by digging into border management. First let's look at borders you can easily control. You will start with your digital space. This is the space you hold in the digital world like on social media platforms. These include Facebook, X, Truth Social, TicTok, and Instagram just to mention a few. These platforms allow you to control who can be in your personal space, what you want the world to see and what you want just your family to see.

Then there is your personal space. This is the space directly around you. This is also easy to control because it is simply the case of letting someone know that they are getting into your space to please take a step back. Now the "simply" part of this isn't always that simple. It's human nature to not easily accept correction. We don't want to be told that we are doing or have done something wrong. For this reason you have to sometimes handle this carefully. There are several general ways to accomplish this. Some people you can just simply let know that they are in your personal space by asking them to step back or using body language to communicate your desire. There are some that you will need to wait until you are in a more private setting before handling it. Then there are also those who no matter how you handle it they will feel offended. This said, you will almost always get some push back, so you have to be prepared to deal with it. You also need to learn that when some one tells you that you are in their personal space to accept this and adjust yourself to keep from crossing their borders.

Now let's look at the borders that can be more difficult to deal with. Let's take the space around your vehicle when you are driving. This is one of the more difficult situations to deal with. Say you are driving behind another vehicle and are about 2 or 3 car lengths behind them. All of the sudden, out of nowhere another vehicle jumps in front of you. I don't know about you but my immediate reaction is anger. How dare somebody do that and get in my personal space. I don't want to drive that close to somebody. The problem is if you slow down a little bit and put more space between you and the new driver in front of you there's a chance another car is going to squeeze in as well. So what do you do, how do you handle it? If you are like most people you will feel the same way at some level and the next few seconds are going to determine how the rest of your day and possibly your life goes. Well let's see what the bible says you should do. How did Jesus handle this type of situation? You can look at Exodus 34 for an answer.

Exodus 34:6

> [6] The LORD passed before him and proclaimed, "The LORD, the LORD, a God merciful and gracious, slow to anger, and abounding in steadfast love and faithfulness,

Notice He says "slow to anger" not "never gets angry". Now this verse in Exodus 34 is just after Moses had received the Ten Commandments for the second time. Moses had brought the first tablets down to the Jews that were in the wilderness and found them partying. They were dancing and sinning and they had made a calf statue out of gold to worship. Moses threw the tablets that God had made and written the Ten Commandments on to the ground and they broke into pieces. Moses was mad and he had destroyed what God had given him to guide His people. He lacked in faith that God had a plan to get His people under control. So Moses had to go back up the mountain to ask God to give him the Ten Commandments again. The difference is this time Moses had to cut the tablets out of stone himself where in the first time God had cut the tablets out of the stone. During this meeting is where God said to Moses the words in Exodus 34:6. So now you see here that although Moses got mad, God showed him grace. He stated that He is "slow to anger" giving you an example of how you need to react when someone encroaches your space. First you have to make sure that they know that there is a price for their actions. Exodus 24 tells you that God gave Moses two tablets with the ten commandments on them. Exodus 34 God has Moses cutting the two tablets of stone and lugging them up the mountain.

Exodus 34:4

> [4] So Moses cut two tablets of stone like the first. And he rose early in the morning and went up on Mount Sinai, as the LORD had commanded him, and took in his hand two tablets of stone.

This time Moses had to work for what God was giving him. Not only did he have to cut them out of stone, he also had to carry them up the mountain. God didn't simply create two more tablets with the Ten Commandments on them. He made sure Moses knew it would take work to implement the commands God was giving to the Israelites. Now it seems that Moses caught on quickly. This time while he was before God he asked Him for help. He asked God to go with him to present the Ten Commandments to the people. God showed great grace and mercy to all the nation by letting them know what He will do for them if they follow the commandments He gave them.

So this was not the only time Moses messes up. Numbers 20 10-13 tells you about another time his in God faith fails. God gave Moses specific instructions so the people could have water. Moses did not follows them but God, who is alway faithful, Still provided the water they needed. But Moses paid for his failure. Open your bible and read this story. I always say that you cannot make a mistake big enough that God can't make good from it.

— Chapter 17 —

It's About Defense Vs Respect

So I touched on the subject earlier asking, what if there are no borders, but there is an understanding that you have your spaces. I then asked the question, Is there really a difference?.

The answer is Yes. There is a big difference. One has you putting your faith in the line that you have drawn identifying your boundaries. The other has you putting your faith in God who will help you manage your boundaries so that his will can be done.

With God managing your boundaries you just have to then take into consideration whether you're encroaching on someone else's boundaries or if someone is encroaching on yours. There is a big difference in this as well. One has you on the inside looking out and the other has you on the outside looking in. It makes sense that if you are on the inside looking out, protecting your spaces, you are on the defense. Ready at any moment to battle anyone who dares to encroach on your space. Whether it is simply someone who stands too close to you or another driver who gets too close to your rear bumper, or gets in front of you, squeezing in between you and the car just ahead of you. God tells us in Luke what to do to those who go against you.

Luke 6:27–29
Love Your Enemies

> [27] "But I say to you who hear, Love your enemies, do good to those who hate you, [28] bless those who

curse you, pray for those who abuse you. [29] To one who strikes you on the cheek, offer the other also, and from one who takes away your cloak do not withhold your tunic either.

How you react to the situation will determine how the other person will react. It's important to have enough faith to believe the other person will understand how they made you feel. The bible in Matthew clearly tells us how to handle these types of situations

Matthew 18:15–17
If Your Brother Sins Against You

> [15] "If your brother sins against you, go and tell him his fault, between you and him alone. If he listens to you, you have gained your brother. [16] But if he does not listen, take one or two others along with you, that every charge may be established by the evidence of two or three witnesses. [17] If he refuses to listen to them, tell it to the church. And if he refuses to listen even to the church, let him be to you as a Gentile and a tax collector.

You have to take into account why they have encroached into your space. If it was done by accident or because they didn't realize they were encroaching into your space you just need to let them know. In most cases they will understand and back off. On the other hand if you react defensively or snap at them they most likely will respond in kind and snap back at you. Having faith is important because with faith you trust.

On the other hand, if you understand each of us has a space that we call our own, and realize you each have your own definition of what that space is, you find yourself on the outside looking in. To not encroach into another person's space will take you to learn how to read others' perspectives of what it means to get too close to their border. Then you need to respect their space and do your best to not enter into it.

So again as I am sitting in Starbucks, I am sitting at the access end of a table for about eight. A gentleman started to go behind me but my chair was blocking the space that he needed to access so he could sit on the same side as I was, which was facing the door. *It's a guy thing because we always want to face the door.* He stopped just as he started to enter but because I was blocking his way and he was going to sit on the other side, with his back to the door. Anyway, I scooted my seat closer to the table to let him in so he could sit where he wanted to. He saw that my personal space was blocking his way in, so he respected it and was willing to not encroach on it. When I pulled my chair in he could see that I didn't mind him passing behind me, so he did. By recognizing each other's personal space everything took place smoothly. We each acted with respect toward each other.

— Chapter 18 —

Bringing it Home

Now that you hopefully have a better understanding of how borders work and what faith truly is, let's bring it home. First of all let's find out what it means to "bring it home". How do you take the faith you have in God, which is weak and failing most of the time, but have enough faith to knock down the borders you have set up here on earth. After all, people and the things you have, let you down all day, every day. Not meaning to most of the time, but purposefully some times.

One of the many hats I wear is that I am a Realtor. I was working a transaction and after looking at dozens of houses my client found the home they wanted. I started talking to the seller's agent and put together an offer to purchase. I discussed it in detail with them and was told that if they made this offer, which was well below what my client was willing to offer, that it would get accepted. On the day the offers were set before the seller I received a call that our offer was not the one selected. Both my buyer and I were shocked. After all, we were assured that our offer would get my buyer the house they wanted. At this point it would seem that we both forgot that God has a grater plan and that His plan is greater than we know. He tells us this in Isaiah.

Isaiah 55:8–9

[8] For my thoughts are not your thoughts, neither are your ways my ways, declares the LORD.

[9] For as the heavens are higher than the earth so are my ways higher than your ways and my thoughts than your thoughts.

So we went on with our search and toured another dozen homes or so. About two weeks into our continued search I received a call from the agent, yes the same one who had let us down. The one who had told me my buyer's offer would get accepted. You will never guess what they told me. Well you probably have already figured it out. The transaction they had going with their client was falling through. They wanted to know if my client was still interested in purchasing the house. So I called my client and they had reservations about it. They were afraid that this agent would let them down again. They had lost faith in them. After all, They had been let down once and did not want to be let down again.

One thing you need to know is that we are both Christians. We both have faith in God, the one who has never let us down. Now don't get me wrong. I did question why God would allow this to happen. After all, He looks out for us and He will never let us down. But He allowed this disappointment to happen and I have to admit that I lost some faith in Him.

Now the seller needed to close by a specific date and that date was closing in fast. Of course this now gave my buyer the advantage. God Never, ever lets you down. Sometimes it may seem like it, but if you keep your faith in Him you can never lose. I have to add that I don't think the agent purposefully misled us. The fact is that it was not in their control at all. It was up to the seller to choose which offer they accepted. It was up to us to have the faith that

God would know the home my buyer wanted and get it for them at a better price. They saved over thirty five thousand dollars from the original offer they were willing to make.

— Chapter 19 —

How Can it Be?

I think that to have faith here on earth you need to really understand God's faith. After all, how can it be that His faithfulness is so perfect? He will never let you down. On the other hand everyone and everything on earth will let you down at some point. Who knows why, but you still sometimes choose to trust the things of this earth more than you trust your Father in heaven who created you. Again you look at Romans 10:17 to see how you can grow in your faith.

Romans 10:17

> [17] So faith comes from hearing, and hearing through the word of Christ.

Since this tells you that "faith comes from hearing" and that "Hearing through the word of Christ", you need to be in God's word and in prayer. When you grow your faith in God you can then share it with others. After all, Christ did command you to share His word with others as told in the Gospels.

Matthew 28:19

> [19] Go therefore and make disciples of all nations, baptizing them in the name of the Father and of the Son and of the Holy Spirit, .

Mark 16:14–16

The Great Commission

[14] Afterward he appeared to the eleven themselves as they were reclining at table, and he rebuked them for their unbelief and hardness of heart, because they had not believed those who saw him after he had risen. [15] And he said to them, "Go into all the world and proclaim the gospel to the whole creation. [16] Whoever believes and is baptized will be saved, but whoever does not believe will be condemned.

So it can be because He died, and defeated death, so that your sins can be forgiven.

— Chapter 20 —

Just Believe

(Have Faith)

It seems to me that if you want to have faith without borders you have to first knock down the boundaries that you allow to exist between you and God. This is done by knowing His word and trusting in Him, That He will never fail us. Matthew, Mark and John all give you an example of what can happen if you knock down the borders you put up between you and Jesus, what can happen if you have full faith in God.

Matthew 14:28-29

> [28] And Peter answered him, "Lord, if it is you, command me to come to you on the water." [29] He said, "Come." So Peter got out of the boat and walked on the water and came to Jesus.

Here Peter is asking Jesus to give him the faith to do the impossible. He sees Jesus walking on water and asks Jesus to prove that He is who He says He is.

Can you just imagine how it would feel to be like Peter as he was walking on water? Have you ever had that much faith?

So there is Peter, walking on water right in front of Jesus. What kind of faith that must take. The wind blowing and the waves slapping around you. Peter then takes his attention off Jesus and the reality of where he is sets in.

Peter's faith begins to fade. As this happened he also began to sink. If you look at the next couple of verses you see this.

Matthew 14:30

> [30] But when he saw the wind, he was afraid, and beginning to sink he cried out, "Lord, save me."

Peter cried out to Jesus to save him. So what did Jesus do? He did what He always does in a situation like this. Let's read on.

Matthew 14:31

> [31] Jesus immediately reached out his hand and took hold of him, saying to him, "O you of little faith, why did you doubt?"

Notice it says how Jesus reacted. Immediately! There was no delay in His response time. Peter saw where Jesus had him, in the midst of the storm. This caused him to start doubting Jesus' power and losing faith. This caused him to start sinking. Have you ever been in a situation like this? How long did you last before you started doubting God's power? Did you cry out to God for help? When you do He will not, He can not ignore us. It's not who He is.

Try to think back of a time you found yourself in this situation. How long did your complete faith hold up? Peter went from having enough faith to do the impossible, to sinking into the rough waters, right there in the face of Jesus. How many times has this happened to you? Do you really want to count?

You know that He will never fail you because His word tells you it is so. Hearing God's word, whether in your mind as you read or have it read aloud to you is what will help you grow in your faith. Then if you live out what is written, others will see this and, if they allow it, their hearts will be softened. Then His word will be etched into their hearts as it says in Ezekiel.

Ezekiel 36:26

> [26] And I will give you a new heart, and a new spirit I will put within you. And I will remove the heart of stone from your flesh and give you a heart of flesh.

Try to imagine that. God pulling out the stone heart that you have and replacing it with a new soft heart that will allow you be open to understanding the words you hear by those who preach. Understanding the words you read in His Holy Word and understanding the words that the Holy Spirit speaks to your heart. It's like all of the sudden the light comes on.

The best analogy I can think of is if you try to walk around in a room that is completely and totally dark. Not one ray of light is cutting through the darkness. You would find yourself bumping into walls and tripping over furniture. Then suddenly the light comes on. Now you can see everything in the room. It makes it possible to walk around without hitting walls and tripping over things.

Several years ago I wrote a personal Psalm about this as I experienced it in my life.

— Chapter 21 —

My Sins Are Greater Than I

My sins are greater than I and fill the room where I am, and the darkness is blacker than the night, but there is nowhere to hide. All light has left my presence and I am like the blind, in a world of darkness. I turn to look but nothing is seen. Where is My God, My Savior, My Redeemer, My Guiding Light? Has He left me? Am I alone on this path? I know from where I came, but do not know to where I go. Why is my journey fruitless? What turn have I taken? Which way should I go? The darkness fills me. It overcomes all that I am. Lord, why have I left your presence? Why did I turn away? How do I get found again? Take from me this cloud that covers the light of Your Son.

I reach out behind where I am and feel a hand. As I turn to see whose it is, the darkness begins to dissolve. The Light begins to return. I again begin to see where I am and where I am going. The more I turn the greater the Light shines. The darkness tries to hide, but it has no place in the Light of the Lord. Your Son stands, outreached hand, waiting. Waiting for me to turn from my misguided ways and return me to the path You have laid for me. With my face to the ground I worship You. I praise You, The Father, The Son and The Holy Spirit. Your grace and mercy have again poured out over me. I am again forgiven.

My Savior will always be. Amen.

Tim Reigle© 2011

Chapter 22

Let's Wrap It Up

Let's have faith without borders

Through your faith in God, His light shines in your heart so you can have faith to trust in Him without the borders that you have set up, to live out His truths and to preach His word. Faith in God's faithfulness that He will never ever let you down, even when you knock down your earthly borders and have faith that He is in command, if you choose to let Him be. Doing this shows the love of Jesus. If someone encroaches on your space, handle it with Love. Respond gently. Let them know how their crossing onto your space makes you feel. Don't get defensive and feel that you need to attack them. Instead cry out to Jesus. He is right there, face to face with you. He will immediately reach out His hand to stop you from sinking just like He did for Peter..

You know that you can't beat God's word into someone's heart, it has to be seen in us. As others see the faith that you have and the fruits of your labor, they too will want to know how this is possible. They will see that you have torn down your borders and that through your faith in God you have faith in them.

This will allow us all to live together, here on earth, and have **Faith Without Borders**.

Matthew 14:25–27

[25] And in the fourth watch of the night he came to them, walking on the sea. [26] But when the disciples saw him walking on the sea, they were terrified, and said, "It is a ghost!" and they cried out in fear. [27] But immediately Jesus spoke to them, saying, "Take heart; it is I. Do not be afraid."

Romans 10:1–4

[1] Brothers, my heart's desire and prayer to God for them is that they may be saved. [2] For I bear them witness that they have a zeal for God, but not according to knowledge. [3] For, being ignorant of the righteousness of God, and seeking to establish their own, they did not submit to God's righteousness. [4] For Christ is the end of the law for righteousness to everyone who believes.

Romans 10:11–13

[11] For the Scripture says, "Everyone who believes in him will not be put to shame." [12] For there is no distinction between Jew and Greek; for the same Lord is Lord of all, bestowing his riches on all who call on him. [13] For "everyone who calls on the name of the Lord will be saved."

Faith Without Borders
What does God say about
the borders you set?
© 2025 Tim Reigle

"Scripture quotations are from the ESV® Bible (The Holy Bible, English Standard Version®), © 2001 by Crossway, a publishing ministry of Good News Publishers. ESV Text Edition: 2025. The ESV text may not be quoted in any publication made available to the public by a Creative Commons license. The ESV may not be translated in whole or in part into any other language. Used by permission. All rights reserved."

Be on the lookout for future books on the subject of faith:

With The Faith of a Child, *How to understand, attain and have faith to live life with the faith of a child.*

Stupid Faith Like David, *How Deep is Your Faith*

And a Fiction" *The Sleepers Amongst Us in 2026*

I Currently have

Arielle Goes to the Park, *Left and Right, Up and Down.*

More books in this children's series are in the works to include *In and Out, Over and Under, Big and Small, Fast and Slow* and *Good and Bad, Right and Wrong.*

Books are currently published through Kindle Direct Print and can be found on amazon.com

To contact the author email Tim at

authortimreigle@gmail.com

About The Author

Tim Reigle first started writing while serving in the United States Army. He took up the hobby of photography and while training he often took pictures to hone his skills. One day a journalist was covering the training for an article in the community newspaper and spotted him taking pictures. He went to him and asked if he was interested in submitting some for possible publication. He was excited to have this opportunity and said "I sure would." He handed the film he had already taken and was given film to shoot more pictures.

Well, low and behold if one of his pictures didn't made the front page of the next edition. He started submitting pictures each time he was in a training exercise. Soon the editor of the paper asked him to write the captions for the photograph's. It wasn't long before that when he was asked to write stories of the training he went on. About a year later he was reassigned to the newspaper as a photojournalist. That planted the seed for Tim's love of using words to tell a story that is intriguing, fun and educating. One thing that helps Tim write good stories is that he has alway lived what he has written about. Whether crawling though the mud with grunts, flying a helicopter or first hand experience in his own life, Tim writes from his heart and what he has lived.

It is hoped that you find his books stimulating, entertaining and educational.

www.ingramcontent.com/pod-product-compliance
Lightning Source LLC
Chambersburg PA
CBHW060846050426
42453CB00008B/853